Move It!

by Becky Manfredini

 HOUGHTON MIFFLIN HARCOURT

PHOTOGRAPHY CREDITS: (c) ©Monalyn Gracia/Fancy/Corbis; 3 ©James Ross/Taxi/Getty Images; 4 ©Jim Vecchi/Corbis Bridge/Corbis; 5 (t) ©matthiasengelien.com/Alamy Images; 7 (tr) ©Photodisc/Getty Images; 8 (b) ©Monalyn Gracia/Fancy/Corbis; 10 (b) ©Loungepark/Digital Vision/ Getty Images

Printed in Mexico

ISBN: 978-0-544-07233-6

9 10 0908 20 19 18 17

4500665006   A B C D E F G

Contents

Vocabulary	Stretch Vocabulary
weather	anemometer
wind	measure
windsock	

Introduction

Describe the weather today. Weather is what the air outside is like. You cannot see air, but you sure can feel it!

Is the air cold or is it hot? Is the air calm or is it windy? Wind is air that moves. You can see tree branches move.

You cannot see wind.

Measuring Wind

Suppose it is a windy day. Go outside. Can you tell where the wind is coming from?

A windsock shows the direction of the wind. Wind enters the windsock at the opening. Then it flows toward the end. The wind is moving in the direction from the opening of the sock to the end.

Without wind, the windsock will not lift up.

The number of an anemometer's spins tells us wind speed.

Do you ever think about how fast the wind is moving? Air can move at different speeds. An anemometer is a tool that measures the speed of wind. It tells us how fast the wind is moving.

The cups on the anemometer catch the moving wind and turn the pole.

Air Can Move Objects

Think about flying a kite on a windy day. The wind catches the kite and lifts it. Then the kite moves up, up, up!

How does a sailboat move in the water? The wind pushes on the sail and moves the boat forward.

What would you do to get this boat to move?

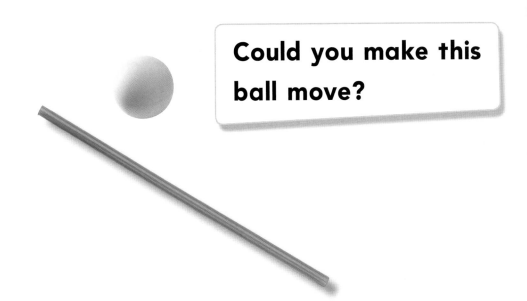

Could you make this ball move?

You might try fanning it with your hand. Next, you might blow on it. But maybe the ball does not move. What would you do next to try to get it to move?

Inside a Bubble

What is light and filled with air? If you said a bubble, you are right! A bubble is round. It is a thin layer of soapy water. Inside the layer is air.

When it is windy, bubbles will move in the direction of the wind.

You blow air into soapy water to make a bubble.

This "empty" cup is actually filled with air.

Inside an Empty Cup

Try this experiment to see another way that air moves.

1. Pour water into a clear container.
2. Turn a tall, empty cup upside down. Push it into the water.
3. Observe that the cup does not totally fill with water.
4. Tilt the cup. Observe that air bubbles rise to the surface of the container.

Tissue-Paper Streamers

Have you ever seen a piece of paper blow around in the wind? In what direction did it blow?

Take some long tissue-paper streamers outside on a windy day. Tape your streamers to a pole or fence.
Ask yourself questions:
In what direction do the streamers move?
Do they all move in the same direction?

Blow on your streamer. How did you make it move?

Balloons get bigger as more air goes in.

Air Is Noisy!

Blowing up a balloon is hard because the balloon has to stretch! If you cannot do it, ask an adult.

Once the balloon is filled with air, let it go. The air inside the balloon will come out. It makes a funny noise and flies around the room! Whoosh! Then the balloon returns to its smaller shape.

Make a Picture List

Go outside on a windy day. Observe objects that move in the wind. Draw a picture of each one. Write the object's name next to each picture.

Write a Shape Poem

A kite goes up in the air on a windy day! Draw a picture of a kite. Write words around the shape of the kite. The words should tell what happens when you fly a kite on a windy day.